Markets of Provence

As a young married couple, Martin and Laurence Toulemonde emerged from the romantic mist of Northern France and headed sunwards to immerse themselves in the delightful cultures of the Mediterranean and Latin America. Having settled in Villeneuve-lès-Avignon some 25 years ago, they have an intimate understanding of both Provence and its natives. They are often joined by Jan and Christina Gabinus, who take every available opportunity to leave their Scandinivian home. Together all four of them have spent the last two years travelling throughout the region selecting the most attractive markets and have united their talents to offer this collection of water-colours, photographs and texts which will help you to discover « les Marchés de Provence ». Martin Toulemonde is also the author of several, illustrated guides for hikers in the Northern Alps.

ISBN 2-7449-0002-8

Martin & Laurence Toulemonde

Markets of Provence

Jan & Christina Gabinus

ÉDISUD

Translated from French by Jean Waegner

Summary

Summary

Introduction

Why not get up one fine morning at the crack of dawn to experience the awakening of a market? In the early morning mist the stallholders, who have long since started their day, take up their allotted spaces under the watchful eye of the market foreman. The cool air is filled with the clinking sound of stalls being set up. The stallholders, who a moment ago were so voluble, are now silent whilst they skilfully arrange their wares following a well-practised routine. Very soon everything is ready. The sun is blazing and the performance can begin. Everyone plays a role: the Provencal with his sing-song way of speaking as well as the holiday-maker in shorts. At the market everyone is relaxed. You are welcomed without formality, gently teased as if you were an old acquaintance and a friendly understanding is arrived at without pomp or ceremony. Social status is forgotten; everyone is equal: the stallholder, the solicitor 's wife and the mayor all shake hands quite freely. So linger and take in the interacting palettes of colours; speak to whomever you please; browse without feeling obliged to buy; listen to the irresistible smooth-talk of the market salesmen or negotiate the price of a live chicken. The prices are not necessarily more reasonable than elsewhere but you know that ever eager to please the "charcutier" and the cheese-seller will make you a present of that little bit extra. Of course much of the produce comes from the wholesale market but you are more likely to respond to those things which hold nostalgic memories of times gone by: the ornate Jerusalem artichoke; the leek still smelling of damp earth; the shiny trail left by a slug on the lettuce still covered with dew; eggs with tiny feathers stuck to them; the sticky humbugs you remember from your childhood and the old trades like that of the knife-grinder or the street busker with his hurdy-gurdy. If your senses are aroused by the interplay of light and colour, you will succumb to the beauty of the shiny red tomatoes which contrast sharply with the pure whiteness of the mushrooms, the warm harmony of the Provencal printed cottons and the sparkling reflection of the glazed pottery under the vast ceiling of the blue sky. Your imagination will wander as you inhale the exotic fragrances of the 'herbes de Provence' and the oriental spices. Soon the clock will strike the hour of retreat and the remaining produce will be hurriedly sold at cut-price. Everything is quickly folded up and everybody scurries home. The market place littered with paper, boxes and straw is handed over to the municipal sweepers.

Allez, les clients, profitez-en, que j'ai tout de beau dans ce livre!

Markets of Provence

Provence is a magical word full of fragrance... but where does Provence begin and end? This question is open to long debate touching many a sensitive point and its roots lie buried in a turbulent and impassioned history.

We have, therefore, courageously evaded the debate and considered, arbitrarily, that Provence has imprecise boundaries which allow it to absorb Uzès and Villeneuve-lès-Avignon although these two towns are indisputably on the right bank of the Rhône, that is to say "off limits". To the south the sea provides an unquestionable frontier whereas to the north we have considered that wherever the olive tree finds its natural habitat qualifies that area to be part of Provence. The most difficult problem is to the east where the mountains of the Dauphiné and the earldom of Nice intermingle with the Alps of Haute Provence. Not being able to make a clear decision, we accept, in advance, any remarks and criticisms that our kind readers might make on this prickly subject.

Compiled in three long chapters, this book sets out on a journey of colourful and fragrant images to discover the most beautiful markets of Provence. You may then make your choice between the numerous weekly markets presented taking care not miss the pages dedicated to the markets of the region which have a special theme and which are one more picturesque than the other.

Part one: The weekly markets.

The weekly markets are held each week throughout the year on the same day and in the same place. From amongst the innumerable markets, we arbitrarily selected those which are generally considered the most colourful either because of their picturesque position or the crowd they draw. Of course, there are other colourful markets that we haven't described. In the large towns there are often several markets sometimes each as attractive as the other; we have limited ourselves to illustrating just one weekly market per town. Each market is designated by the name of the town, the area or village in which it is found and the "département" in which it is situated.

The map on page 50 indicates the location of the weekly markets which we have described and illustrated.

You will find the markets grouped according to the day of the week on which they take place. If a weekly market takes place on more than one day of the week, it is classified under the day on which it is the most important. If a market is held daily, it is classified under the heading "everyday".

A colour, which appears in the title, symbolises each day of the week.

Monday		Tuesday	
Wednesday		Thursday	
Friday		Saturday	
Sunday		Everyday	

The other important markets that we haven't described are, however, mentioned at the beginning of the chapter, in the water-colour margin.

The weekly markets always offer fresh food, mainly fruit and vegetables but also usually cheeses, olive oil, olives and home-made "tapenade" (olive paste), meat, "charcuterie", fish and shell-fish as well as articles of clothing and shoes. Most of the time you will also find flowers, honey and nougat, wine sold in bulk, books and discs, basket-work, hardware, crockery and "artisanat" (handmade and home-made) articles. This list is far from being exhaustive as you can find almost anything at a weekly market: furniture, medicinal herbs, live trout, faith-healers surrounded by lucky charms or serpents' skins, haberdashery and sewing machines, articles for hunting or fishing, chair upholsterers, knife-grinders, cobblers and hurdy-gurdy players....

Furthermore, you will also find symbols which give an estimate of the relative importance of certain features notably the size, presence or absence of a particular type of merchandise. This information is only an indication; for example it cannot take into account the important differences you may notice at a market depending on whether your visit is in summer or in winter. However, these symbols should enable you to make a comparison of a market in relationship with the others.

You will encounter
3 symbols showing "size":
quite small, medium, quite large

3 symbols showing "bags":
rather a small amount of food-stuffs on offer, a medium amount, a good variety of food-stuffs on offer

3 symbols showing "clothing":
not many clothing articles, a medium amount, a lot of clothing articles on offer

3 symbols showing "pottery":
not much "artisanat", some "artisanat", a lot of "artisanat" on offer

3 symbols showing "flowers":
not many flowers, some flowers, lots of flowers on offer

a symbol showing "a chicken":
possibility of buying live animals.

Finally, to indicate whether a market is more or less picturesque and whether it will provide the opportunity to take interesting photos, you will find the following symbols:

3 symbols showing "rolls of film":
quite picturesque, of medium interest, very picturesque

As weekly markets are mostly held in the morning, you will have time after the market to explore the surroundings. We have thus indicated, by way of suggestion, certain historic, artistic or touristic centres of interest which merit a visit once the markets have taken down their parasols. For more details on these propositions, contact the tourist offices.

NB:
"Charcuterie" (cured meats and sausages)
"Artisanat" (handmade or home-made goods)

Part two: Fairs and Markets with a special theme.

The markets having a special theme also take place in the open air but they are devoted to the sale of only one product. The best example is the fish market in Marseille which is held each day on the quai des Belges at the far end of the old port. The flea markets, flower markets, truffle markets, the horse fairs or the "santon" markets are also markets with a special theme. For each theme we have indicated the locations and the dates we judge most worthy of interest but once again the abundance of such markets prevented us from making a complete list.

The fairs or festivals take place once a year in a specific place. As with the special markets they only deal with one product. There may be several fairs for any one product. For example the Piolenc garlic fair and the one on the Cours Belsunce in Marseille. They can also be unique as is the linden blossom fair in Buis-les-Baronnies. We have endeavoured to give you an indication of the main fairs in Provence but not all have been mentioned. The dates of the fairs may vary according to the civil or church calendar. Before you set out it is advisable to check it exists as well as its exact date by asking at the town-hall or tourist office.
The map on page 94 indicates the special markets, fairs or festivals illustrated in Part two.

Discovering the markets of Provence

Rognes

Toulon

54 Kg
28. Kg

Arles

Graveson

Aix-en-Provence

Marseille, les Capucins

Gordes

Reillanne

Apt

Aubagne

Marseille, Vieux-Port

PRUNES
MACH 1003

Grasse

Villeneuve-lez-Avignon

Saint-Tropez

Martigues

L'Isle-sur-la-Sorgue

Carpentras

Sardu · Salée
48,00 Fr/Kg

Fontvieille

Saint-Tropez

Avignon

Aix-en-Provence

L'Isle-sur-la-Sorgue

PAIN DE FROMENT
PUR LEVAIN NATUREL
22 Fr LE KG

SAUCISSON
AUX
OLIVES

Toulon

Avignon

Arles

Toulon

Apt

Sénas

Riez

L'Isle-sur-la-Sorgue

L'Isle-sur-la-Sorgue

Vaison-
la Romaine
Mont-Ventoux
Orange
Sault
Carpentras
Uzès
Forcalquie
Reillanne
Villeuve
lèz-Avignon
L'Isle-sur
la-Sorgue
Gordes
Apt
La Tour d'Aig
Avignon
Cavaillon
Lourmarin
Tarascon
Les Alpilles
Pertuis
Arles
Salon-
de-Provence
Aix-en-Provence
Saintes-Maries
de-la-Mer
Martigues
Aubag
Marseille

Les Alpes
The weekly markets
Riez
Aups
Grasse
tagne
-Victoire
Massif des Maures
Saint-Tropez
Toulon

The weekly markets

Monday

VAUCLUSE
Bédarrides
Bédoin
Bollène
Cadenet
Cavaillon
Piolenc
Saint-Didier

BOUCHES-DU-RHÔNE
Fontvieille* (summer)
Fuveau*
La Destrousse
Saintes-Maries-de-la-Mer*
Venelles

VAR
La Valette*
Les Issambres

ALPES DE HAUTE-PROVENCE
Barrême (summer)
Forcalquier

DRÔME PROVENÇALE
La-Motte-Chalancon (summer)
Tulette

**twice weekly market*

Cavaillon

The area of Cavaillon is the garden of Provence (...) here an amazing quantity of artichokes, peas, garlic and excellent fruit, especially peaches, are gathered. The inhabitants make good use of every small corner of their land. By their labour and with the help of the fertiliser procured from the silt-laden waters of the Durance they exploit the precious soil and contribute to the riches of the region. This text, written many years ago, acknowledges the old established horticultural tradition of the plain of Cavaillon which is irrigated by water from the mill reaches and protected from the mistral by the St. Jacques hill. Today, the melon having found here the right conditions for its flourishing growth has made Cavaillon famous. This "slice of honey" truly evokes the sweet warmth of the Provencal summer, the shrill song of the cicadas and the far off bluish tint of the Luberon. The abundance and quality of the produce from the market gardens is found in the market every Monday morning. In the old town, the food stalls are set up under the shade of the plane trees next to the Roman arcades of the cathedral, whereas, in front of the Roman triumphal arch, a whole road is given over to articles of clothing, shoes and agricultural implements. In summer a "marché Provencal "lasts all day and in Coustellet there is a "marché paysan" (local producers market) every Sunday morning.

After the market do not miss:

in Cavaillon, the cathedral St. Véran and its cloister, the Roman triumphal arch, the synagogue (XV and XVIII century).
a walk up the St. Jacques hill (also possible by car) and an absolutely magnificent view of the town, the Rhône and Durance valleys and the Luberon Mountains.
the string of pretty villages which surround the Luberon.
walks along the footpaths of the Luberon.

Saintes-Maries de la Mer

The international fame which the Camargue enjoys makes those, who long for large open spaces, converge on Les Saintes-Maries-de-la Mer. There they abandon themselves to their dreams whilst observing the migratory birds passing by. It also attracts all those who love the unspoilt nature for which it is renowned and typified by the white Camargue horses, the black "toros" (bulls) and the pink flamingoes. After having crossed miles of paddy fields studded with white thatched-roofed cottages, the road stops at Saintes-Marie-de-la-Mer, a pretty village clustered around its extraordinary fortified Romanesque church, the Mecca of religious devotion for gypsies from all parts of Europe, which is crammed with naive and moving ex-votos. The church tower dominates the market square. During the summer months the stalls are set out in a square around an open space of golden sand which reflects the dazzling sunlight. These stalls have obviously been conceived to appeal to holiday-makers and you will also find many more "artisans" than elsewhere dressed up in traditional costume. All of go to lengths to give themselves either a Camargue, Provencal or exotic look in order to make those from the North dream and blink with delight under the Mediterranean sun.

After the market do not miss:

a tour of the fortified church and the very beautiful view of the Camargue and the sea from the roof top path
the Baroncelli museum dedicated to the Camargue
the Pont de Gau ornithological park (the best period is at the time of the migrations in October and March)
Aigues-Mortes, the ramparts and the tower of Constance
The château d' Avignon on the road to Arles
The little Camargue railway.

Forcalquier

Our Lady of the Market, the melodies of the hurdy-gurdy flow like the lively waters of the Durance and, in the upper part of the town, on the Place St. Michel, in front of the famous, libidinous bas-relief, biologically produced fruit and vegetables exude freshness.

After the market do not miss:

The Notre Dame de Salagon priory.
Sauvan castle.
The Abbey of Ganagobie (12th century).
The old villages of Lurs, Dauphin, Vachères, Oppedette, Simiane-la-rotonde.
Rambles in the Lure mountain, the Luberon or the Oppedette canyon.
Cycle ride on the cycle path towards Cereste and Apt.
The lavender fields on the plateau of Valensole (in bloom beginning of July).

"The homo-ecologicus" chose to settle down in Forcalquier. He speaks French with the local accent, English, Dutch or gibberish. He wears clothes in ecru and natural colour patch-work, carries his baby on his back or in front of him and has tufts of matted hair peeping from under a strange hat. He is laid back and friendly. The Monday morning market, which he frequents regularly, provides authenticity. The cured ham is from wild boar, the pullovers are the same colours as the sheep from the Lure mountain, bread is made from cracked wheat, the "herbes de Provence" have not had far to come to get to the market, the lavender from the Valensole plateau spreads its subtle, delicious, perfume over the stalls and the "arti-sanaux" products are found in abundance. In front of the door to the cathedral, dedicated to

Tuesday

VAUCLUSE
Caderousse
Cucurron
Gordes
La Tour-d'Aigues
Saint-Saturnin-les-Apt
Sarrians*
Vaison-la-Romaine

BOUCHES-DU-RHÔNE
Aubagne
Eguilles
Istres
Le Tholonet*
Tarascon

VAR
Cotignac (summer)

ALPES DE HAUTE-PROVENCE
Banon
Gréoux-les-Bains*
Les Mées*

DRÔME PROVENÇALE
Grignan
La Bégude de Mazenc
Saint-Paul-Trois-Châteaux

**twice weekly market*

Aubagne

Aubagne is the kingdom of the santons (crib figures). The exceptional purity of the local clay attracted the santon craftsmen to settle down in Aubagne. Every day in December and during the summer "santons" can be found at the big weekly market held on Wednesdays. Every other year, potters from the whole region assemble in Aubagne for "Argila", the biggest pottery market in Europe (15th August). In the old town, nestled into the hillside, the streetlamps throw dark arabesque shadows on the warm ochre coloured facades as the sun caresses the superb decor, made of monochrome earthenware tiles, which adorn the ancient washing-place.

The market is held at the foot of the hill. The fruit, vegetable and flower stalls are clustered around coloured parasols with the old town, dominated by its church steeple and belltower as a backdrop. The town has clearly inspired the decor of the cribs for the "santons". Here the incantations of Pagnol, a native of Aubagne, find their natural setting. The scents of the garrigue envelope the neighbouring hills and the characteristic silhouette of the Garlaban stands out above the rooftops. On the other side of the Cours Maréchal Foch second- hand clothing stalls, haberdashers and shoe and hat salesmen are to be found. When it is hot, the thirsty customers relax on the numerous animated café terraces under the shade of the magnolia trees and enjoy the show while sipping a suitably chilled pastis.

After the market do not miss:

the Marcel Pagnol circuit
the small world of Marcel Pagnol, esplanade de Gaulle
the old town with its multicoloured facades, its churches and the workshop Th. Neveu
a santon or pottery workshops
the Foreign Legion museum
Cassis and a boat trip to the calanques (creeks) or on foot for the sportsmen

Gordes

Gordes resembles a Provencal crib village or is it that the crib villages are often modelled on this pretty village, compacted on a promontory around the crenellated walls of its castle. A market, much appreciated in all seasons, is held in the square on Tuesday mornings. Right at the beginning of summer, all those who have suffered a long, foggy winter dream of immersing themselves in the luminous Provençal countryside and of falling under the irresistible charm of the Luberon, the fragrance of its slopes and the winding alleyways of its old villages. The market in Gordes generously offers them the fragrances of thyme, melon and figs; the rude remarks and singing intonations of the Provençal market folk; the shimmering light on the surface of the glazed pottery or on the ancient stones of the keep; and the bluish horizons outlined by the backbone of the mountain above the valley of Coulon. At a stone's throw from the market, the works of the artist Vasarely hang from the picture-rails in the castle putting together a world of colours and changing the defensive architecture of the building into a Mecca of the most advanced kinetic art.

What to see in the surroundings:

The abbey of Sénanque (XII century)
The village of the "Bories"
The Luberon mountain and its string of old villages
Fontaine-de-Vaucluse, the mysterious resurgence of the river Sorgue
The "Colorado Provencal", quarries of multicoloured ochre

Tarascon

Made famous by the "Tarasque" a legendary monster which devoured man and beast alike and by Alphonse Daudet's Tartarin, the bragging lion-hunter who, if the mistral was blowing, would not venture onto the bridge across the Rhône except on all fours, Tarascon, with its many roundabouts embellished with magnificent flower-beds still proudly boasts its castle on the river bank. The Languedoc river bank is held by Beaucaire which, from the middle-ages until the birth of the railway, was the centre for the fabulous trade fairs. Carts and boats brought silk from Lyon, soap from Marseille, wool and skins from the Camargue, cloth from Holland, lace from Calais, cereals from Piémont, swords from Toledo as well as exotic produce such as coffee, sugar, cinnamon and cocoa. The market in Tarascon today still reflects this intermingling of races and French, Arabic and Spanish are spoken in almost equal proportions.

An enormous choice of clothing articles can be found on the circular boulevard around Tarascon and the fresh fruit and flowers on offer enhance the old streets inside the town-walls leading up to the pretty arcades and the townhall's imposing facade.

After the market do not miss:

The castle and the magnificent view from its high towers.
The Souleiade private museum (by appointment 04 90 91 05 08).
The Montagnette hills, the abbey of St. Michel-de-Frigolet and the château at Barbentane.
The troglodytic fortress abbey of St. Roman.
In Graveson, the museum of aromas and perfumes and the museum of the Provencal artist, Chabaud.
Fontvieille and the mill of Alphonse Daudet.

La Tour-d'Aigues

Striking and solemn Renaissance ruins warmly illuminated by the morning sun - what a strange and rare setting for a country market! The architecture as a whole seems incomplete and dates from the years 1550 - 1580. The castle, built on the foundations of an ancient fortification, was bought in 1719 by the tyrannical Jérome de Bruni who loved art and earthenware so much that he set up a factory workshop in his castle. However, prior to the revolution which was to break out some years later, the people, who were exhausted from being exploited by the aristocracy, set fire to the castle in 1780 and for good measure plundered it and set fire to it again in 1792. A tall story was spread by bad-intentioned inhabitants of neighbouring villages that a villager from Tourain, who was a prisoner in the castle jail, got his head stuck between the bars of his cell thus earning the inhabitants of la Tour-d' Aigues the reputation of having "big heads but little brain". In any case, little does this matter, embellished as it is by the presence of these majestic ruins, the market has an aristocratic feeling about it which makes it stand out from other markets which are less endowed.

After the market do not miss:

The museum of the history of the region of Aigues and of earthenware situated in the castle's cellar.
The village of Ansouis, its old church, castle and gardens.
A ramble in the gorge of Régalon in the Luberon.
The chateau of Lourmarin: in summer, cultural events, exhibitions and concerts.

Vaison-la-Romaine

For over 2000 years the village centre has moved from one side of the river Ouvèze to the other side and the market of Vaison-la-Romaine, like the rest of the town, has drifted from the right river bank to the foot of the castle on the left bank. All year through it hosts a very important market, attracting most of the local population as well as that of Nyons and the Baronnies. One can always find bargains at this big market a famous example being that of the collector who, in 1870, traded a case of silkworm cocoons for fragments of a Roman statue of Diadumenos which he then sold to the British Museum in London for 25,000 francs. In summer, the combined effect of holiday-makers, the return of people who have second homes in the area and the presence of singers from choirs (every 3 years) renders the market even more lively. During the estival season there is a "Marché Provencal" on Sunday in the upper town and on Tuesday, Wednesday and Saturday there is a small market for local producers.

After the market do not miss:

A visit to the Roman ruins, the town and the theatre.
A tour of the Dentelles de Montmirail, walks around the old villages, rock climbing.
A tour of the vineyards' cellars of Vacqueyras, Gigondas, Beaumes-de-Venise.
Walks in the hills around Nyons and the Baronnies or in the Toulourenc river bed.

Wednesday

VAUCLUSE
Châteauneuf-de-Gadagne
Gargas
Le Thor*
Malaucène
Mallemort-du-Comtat
Mérindol
Sault
Valréas*

BOUCHES-DU-RHÔNE
Cassis*
Orgon
Rognes
Salon-de-Provence*
Saint-Rémy-de-Provence

VAR
Bormes-les-Mimosas
Cavalaire (summer)
Cogolin (summer)
Draguignan*
La Crau
Salernes*
Sanary-sur-mer
Solliès-Pont
Saint-Maximin

ALPES DE HAUTE-PROVENCE
Digne
Riez
Sisteron

DRÔME PROVENÇALE
Buis-les-Baronnies
Montélimar*
Rémuzat

**twice weekly market*

Buis-les-Baronnies

European capital of the lime or linden tree, Buis-les-Baronnies produces nine-tenths of all the linden blossom harvested in France thanks to the 30,000 trees accounted for in the region. Also, here all other aromatic herbs such as lavender, thyme, savory or rosemary find favourable growing conditions. The olive tree, the vine and the apricot tree obviously like the conditions too. Being very close to the Mont-Ventoux, when in summer all the Provence plain seeks shade, it is an oasis of greenery, freshness and a clear sky. Thanks to its hillyness it is protected from the great migrations of tourists and this pretty village has conserved all of its authenticity and immense charm. Those who have discovered it keep the closely guarded secret for fear of drawing the crowds and they remain attached to it forever. They can be found every Wednesday morning in front of the stalls set up around the irregular arcades of the market place (XV century) or on the esplanade under the plane trees planted in 1811 to commemorate the birth of the king of Rome. Considering the size of the village, the market is very important because it draws the population of a number of miniscule hamlets scattered in the mountains. Here they enjoy the opportunity to meet with friends and acquaintances whilst replenishing their baskets for the week. Craftsmen, who have found here an ideal place for working in peace, add in their own way a touch of beauty and originality. It is on la Place de Quinconce, under the shade of trees which are more than a hundred years old, that this extraordinary linden blossom market is held on the first Wednesday in July.

After the market do not miss:

La maison des arômes (house of aromas) on the bank of the Ouvèze.
The olive mill in the village.
Wide choice of walks in the hills or in the Toulourenc river bed.
The old village of Brantes at the foot of the Mont-Ventoux.

Riez

Until quite recently, life in Riez flowed along at a gentle pace dictated by the rhythm of the farming year and the activities of hatters, potters and makers of pasta. The annual three day "fête de la bravade" at Whitsun during which the air was rent by hundreds of pounds of gunpowder being exploded, heralded the start of the wheat and lavender harvests. In those days, peace reigned beneath the beating sun in the Colostre valley and the sundial on la Place Saint-Antoine evoked philosophical thoughts by indicating nostalgically that "the most serene moment is marked by a shadow". The four columns of the ancient Gallo-Roman city and the old baptistery dating from the fourth century were not enough to draw the crowds. However, our leisure-seeking society has changed all that. The plateau of Valensole covered with fields of lavender, Moustiers-Sainte-Marie and its celebrated decorated earthenware, the gorges of Verdon and the lake of Sainte-Croix are now confirmed tourist attractions and the Wednesday and Saturday morning markets have become amongst the most appreciated attractions.

After the market do not miss:

A walk in the alley-ways of the old town or to the Mont St. Maxime.
The monolithic columns of the ancient Gallo-Roman city.
The Merovingian baptistery and the lapidary museum.
Moustiers-Sainte-Marie and its decorated earthenware.
The awe-inspiring cliff road of the "grand canyon" of Verdon and the lake Sainte-Croix.

Sault

In France the year 1515 is normally associated with the battle of Marignan. However, in Sault they have an even better reason to remember 1515 as it was the year that the Count of Sault decreed there would be a market every Wednesday morning. The town is on a promontory and when you wander round the market the view you have extends over the colourful undulations of the plateau and to the summit of the Mont-Ventoux which is often peaked with snow. It is considered to be the place to go for a good chat by the isolated inhabitants of the immense Vauclusien plateau who love to meet up with each other here every week. In summer, when the valley of the Rhone is stifling, the altitude of the plateau preserves a mild and delightful temperature. The lavender, which embalms the air and whose violet rows accentuate the contours of the hills is a much discussed topic. In winter, you can settle down in the sun, sheltered from the mistral wind, to discuss the last wild boar hunt or the shooting of thrushes which, by special dispensation, may be pursued until the end of February.

After the market do not miss:

An outing by car or on foot in the Nesque gorges.
The Mont-Ventoux.
The lavender route (in bloom in July) and the garden of lavenders in the hamlet of Verdolier.
An outing to the valley of the Toulourenc passing through Aurel and Brantes.

Culinary specialities:

Dark or white nougat, macaroons.
Potters' market at the lavender festival on the 15th August.

Saint-Rémy-de-Provence

Although he was a remarkable clairvoyant, Nostradamus, who was born here, does not appear to have been able to foresee the success that this little town was going to acquire.
Set in the verdant countryside and dominated by the elegant profile of the Alpilles, St. Rémy-de -Provence is coiled up lying dormant and full of charm, in the middle of the road which encircles it, snug like a cat in its basket. Every Wednesday morning, the village is overrun by a market which brings colour to the roads, the squares and the winding alleys. The sunlight mixes with the golden olive oil, the amber-coloured honey and the crimson aubergines to create pictures worthy of Van Gogh, who lived here at the end of his life. Even though his Basque beret is rather unexpected, the "charcutier" from the Landes region will enchant you by serving you a small glass of wine whilst you taste his "terrine" ! Under the Tricolour flags flying from the townhall, two little girls pertinently comment on the fragrance of thyme and rosemary whilst the street-singer gaily turns the handle of his hurdy-gurdy.

After the market do not miss:

Glanum and other Roman ruins.
Les-Baux-de-Provence and the cathedral of images.
A walk to the little lake of St. Rémy.
A walk in the Alpilles.
In season, organ concerts in the church of St. Martin.

Thursday

VAUCLUSE
Cairanne
Caumont-sur-Durance
Le Pontet
Orange
Roussillon (summer)
Vacqueyras

BOUCHES-DU-RHÔNE
Auriol
Martigues
Maussane (summer)

VAR
Les Arcs
Carqueiranne
Grimaud (summer)
Ollioules*
Rians
Villecroze

ALPES DE HAUTE-PROVENCE
Allemagne-en-Provence
Gréoux-les-Bains*
Les Salles-sur-Verdon

DRÔME PROVENÇALE
Nyons*
Rochegude

GARD
Villeneuve-lez-Avignon*

**twice weekly market*

Martigues

Resting on the water between the Mediterranean sea and the Etang de Berre, Martigues is an amphibious town which mirrors itself in its canals. Under the graceful movements of the gulls, the very well named, "Miroir aux Oiseaux" reflects the shimmering, upside-down images of the boat hulls and that of the Madeleine cathedral. Well before you, this spectacle fascinated Delacroix, Dufy, Corot, Picabia, Ziem and many others. Canals, bridges, quays and gangways are a permanent reminder that the town belongs to both the water and the land. The market is no exception to this rule. The stalls of fruit and vegetables rise above the rounded shapes of the small boats and the flower-sellers are reflected in the still waters of the canal. The island is too small to accommodate the entire market so it has gone across the water to invade the banks of the "étang" at Joncquières. One would expect to find fish everywhere in such an aquatic surrounding but it is clothing stalls which occupy the greatest area along the palm trees and the flower-beds of the quai des Anglais.

After the market do not miss:

The "Miroir aux Oiseaux" (mirror of the birds).
The Ziem museum.
The chapel of the Annonciade.
Panorama from the chapel of Notre-Dame-des-Marins.
The creeks of the Côte Bleue.

Nyons

"Nyons to me is paradise on earth"
(Giono)

Famous for its apricots, olives and oil, the town of Nyons, well protected from the indomitable mistral wind, stretches out in the sun between palm trees and olive trees. Here, the olive is so important that the region of Nyons was the first to obtain an "appellation d'origine controllée" for its olives and olive oil. The tasting of the new oil in February, gives rise to an eccentric festival, the "alicoque". On the village square everyone is invited to taste a small toasted crouton which has been rubbed with garlic and soaked in the new olive oil. In winter, the Thursday market is confined to three squares at the end of the town. In summer, it invades all the shaded alleyways and for good measure a "marché Provencal" is held every Sunday morning near the elegant, dissymmetric arch of the Roman bridge which boldly straddles the Eygues. On the other side of the river, between the Baronnies hills, the harmonious disorder of the little patchwork plots of land is a feast for the eye. The lines of the large, dark trunks of the hundred year old olive trees bear bouquets of brilliant, quivering leaves. The rows of vines emphasise the contours of the hills and, at the end of winter, the orchards of apricot trees decorate the banks of the blue-tinted course of the river Eygues.

After the market do not miss:

La rue des grands-forts, the old staircase alleyways.
The Roman bridge and, at the foot of the bridge, the olive oil mill (with video presentation).
The garden of aromas.
The old village of St-May and the gorges of the Eygues.
A walk in the Baronnies hills.
The Roman ruins of Vaison-la-Romaine.

Orange

The magnificent Roman theatre, the triumphal arch and the ruins of the Roman gymnasium testify to the importance of the town in Roman times and justify the fame of Orange and its theatre festival. After the "pax romana", the events of history gave rise to the construction of the circular ramparts. These, when destroyed, were replaced by the large avenues of plane trees, the perfect place for the market which has been taking place in Orange on every Thursday morning since the year 1428. Today, the big market which has retained all the best traditions of the past, is still an important weekly event. One comes here as much to do the shopping as to discuss the strength of the mistral, to have knives sharpened, to joke with the sea-urchin salesman or to taste the wine drawn from the barrel. Under the plane trees of the avenues and alleys, the Mediterranean nuances of the freshly painted facades evoke the thousand colours of the market: the blue of the fresh sardines, the red of the coral grouper fish, the yellow of the Spanish melons, the marbled tints of the strange gourds and the ochre of the chestnut leaf wrapped round the Banon cheese.

After the market do not miss:

The Roman theatre and triumphal arch.
Châteauneuf-du-pape, its vineyards, wine cellars, vine museum of Father Anselme.
Sérignan du Comtat, former home of the entomologist Jean-Henri Fabre.
Outings in the Dentelles de Montmirail.

Villeneuve-lez-Avignon

In the past an old rivalry brought Villeneuve-lès-Avignon and Avignon into conflict, each one pretending to be on the best side of the Rhône. One side belonged to the pope and the other to the king of France. In order to cross the St. Bénézet bridge, the famous bridge of Avignon on which everyone dances according to the popular song, credentials had to be shown as, on the French side, it was guarded by the army at the Philippe-le-Bel tower and on the papal side by the fortifications of Avignon. The leather fair was held in both towns on the same day, each town trying to outdo the other. Times have long since changed. Both towns are now nested in the bosom of the same republic and everyone thinks of Villeneuve as a charming, little Provencal town although it is effectively in Languedoc. The Thursday market occupies a vast esplanade, an ancient orchard that le Puy-Andaon cliff, surmounted by the fort St. André, tries in vain to shelter from the mistral. The most pleasant way of getting to the market is to descend on foot from the fort St. André by taking the well named "rue Pente Rapide" (rapid slope) which gives you a simultaneous view of the popes' palace, the Philippe-le-Bel tower and the multicoloured parasols of the market.
On Saturday morning there is a "marché Provencal" on the Place Jean Jaures and a flea market on the Place du Marché.

After the market do not miss:

The fort St. André, its abbey, gardens and towers.
At the Pierre-de-Luxembourg museum, the famous Coronation of the Virgin by Enguerrand Quarton, and the statue of the Virgin in polychrome ivory.
The collegiate church and its cloister.
The tower Philippe-le-Bel, the old toll-gate at the entrance to the bridge of Avignon and the lovely exhibitions which are held here.
The park behind the school with its magnificent view of Villeneuve and of the Mont-Ventoux.

Friday

VAUCLUSE
Bonnieux
Carpentras
Châteauneuf-du-Pape
Lagnes
Lourmarin
Pertuis

BOUCHES-DU-RHÔNE
Carry-le-Rouet*
Graveson (summer)
Gréasque*
Mallemort
Mouriès (summer)
Roquevaire
Saint-Martin-de-Crau

VAR
Le Beausset*
La Capte (summer)
La Garde*
Le Pradet*
Rians

ALPES DE HAUTE-PROVENCE
Moustiers-Sainte-Marie

DRÔME PROVENÇALE
Dieulefit
Pierrelatte
Suze-la-Rousse
Taulignan

**twice weekly market*

La Capte

To adapt itself to the narrowness of the isthmus on which it is set up, La Capte's summertime Friday market has adopted an enormous spaghetti-like shape spreading out over almost two kilometres, in the shade of the pine trees which line the large, sandy beaches. Needless to say everything is done to accommodate the holiday-makers who have come to relax. Amongst other things, one can find swimsuits of all shapes and colours, which can be tried on behind a bamboo curtain where one conceals oneself as best as possible, sandals and beach-shoes, Provençal skirts and Polynesian wrap-arounds and, for the picnic, pizzas and paellas to take away, watermelons, melons and trays of peaches and local cheeses and "charcuterie". The stallholder assures you "c' est pas de la drouille, que du bon produit!" ("its not just any old rubbish, it's the genuine article!"). Of course, all the local "artisanat" work is also on offer for you to take home as a souvenir of your holiday or to give as presents to the friends with whom you are staying. Everyone is relaxed, smiling and tanned. Allow yourself to wander from one end of this seemingly never-ending market to the other. This might take a bit of time, but then again, you are not in a hurry.

After the market do not miss:

A boat trip to Porquerolles or Port-Cros.
A walk along the customs footpath which starts at La Madrague.
A visit to Saint-Tropez along the coastal road of Maures.

Carpentras

The market of Carpentras owes its good fortune to the Count of Toulouse, who accorded it, in 1155, the monopoly of markets between Orange, Vaison-la-Romaine and l'Isle-sur-Sorgue. No other village in this region had the right to hold a market concurrently. Being directly interested in the development of business affairs, the bishop, and then the pope, established an extraordinarily complicated tax system and controlled by threat of excommunication and dispensation of indulgences the Friday markets and the large fairs of Saint Matthieu and Saint Siffrein. The presence of jews, tolerated in Carpentras where they fulfilled the function of bankers, equally contributed to the expansion of the market. The woad used to dye materials indigo was sold here, presented in conical forms called "cocagnes" which enriched its manufacturers so much that "pays de cocagne" became the synonym for a region of plenty. Also found here were enormous quantities of saffron stamens, the reddish pigment from the madder plant, tobacco, skeins and cocoons of silk, truffles, wool, woollen cloth and tanned skins. Today, Friday sees all the roads and alleys of Carpentras invaded by a colourful, jabbering crowd. In winter, the truffles embalm the air in front of the bar de l'Univers. In spring, the Carpentras strawberry has no problem eliminating its Moroccan and Spanish rivals and the flower-stalls, under the plane trees in the avenue Jean-Jaures, rightly claim fame throughout the region.

After the market do not miss:

L'Hôtel-Dieu and its collection of apothecary earthenware.

The synagogue, one of the oldest and most beautiful in France.

The Dentelles of Montmirail: walks here are superb in all seasons.

Lourmarin

Honoured with the title "the most beautiful village in France", Lourmarin occupies the strategic point where the Loube, after having cut its way through the Luberon, gains the wide valley of the Durance. Its castle projects its look-out towers into the clear blue sky making it difficult to imagine that this pleasant and peaceful village was once the object of a terrible persecution. In 1545, having been won over by the Vaudois convictions, which the Catholic church considered as heretical, men, women and children were massacred together with those from eleven neighbouring villages. The memory of the Vaudois is still alive but since those times a lot of the Loube's water has flowed under the bridge, the Provence sun has erased all the blood and tears and a smile has reappeared on everyoneís lips. Every Friday morning the stalls are set up for the pretty "marché Provençal". Whether a tourist passing through or a Provencal from old stock, here everyone finds their own contentment in a peaceful, good-natured atmosphere. The "artisans" set up their stalls alongside the other traders and will repair any Provencal chairs you may possess with deft craftsmanship.

After the market do not miss:

The well set out walk around the village.
The magnificent clock-tower nicknamed "boîte à sel".
The fountains built over the centuries.
The restored Romanesque church.
The castle, "Villa Médicis de Provence".

Pertuis

Pertuis (meaning passage) is a transit town between the Rhône-Durance basin and the Alps and is a magnet of attraction for the whole region as the importance of its Friday market clearly demonstrates. A large car-park, situated at the end of the old town, allows easy access on foot to the centre of the village, which is completely taken over by the weekly market. The Place Mirabeau is dominated by the elegant campanile of the St. Jacques tower and embraces the white parasols of the most picturesque part of the market situated in front of the porch of the church of St. Nicolas. A large fountain and the terraces of several bistros complete the charm of this square. The straight rows of stalls stretch out along the whole length of the Cours de la République. The passage left free for the customers is so narrow that it puts off those in a hurry but is a joy to those who are happy to go along at an easy pace.

After the market do not miss:

The old town, the organs in the church of St. Nicolas (historic monument), the doors and the old ramparts.
Ansouis, its castle and amazing church of St. Martin.
The rooftops of Cucuron viewed from the keep's terrace.
The Vaudois village of St. Martin-de-la-Brasque.
The ruins of the Renaissance castle in La-Tour-d'Aigues.

"Marché Provencal" Wednesday and Saturday morning, Place Garcin.
Horse-fair in June.
Flower market at the beginning of May.

Saturday

VAUCLUSE

Apt
Jonquières
Le Thor*
Mornas
Oppède-le-Vieux (summer)
Pernes-les-Fontaines
Richerenches

BOUCHES-DU-RHÔNE

Arles
Auriol*
Carnoux*
Charleval
Marignane
Plan-de-Cuques
Saint-Chamas

VAR

Aups*
Barjoles
Brignoles
Saint-Tropez
Fayence*
Fréjus*
Hyères
Tourtour*

ALPES DE HAUTE-PROVENCE

Cruis
Manosque
Castellane (summer)

DRÔME PROVENÇALE

Crest* (**)
Donzère
Montrond-les-Bains
Sauzet

GARD

Pont-Saint-Esprit
Uzès

ALPES-MARITIMES

Grasse*

**twice weekly market*
***evening market, 3 times in summer*

Apt

If you leave behind the green valley of the Rhône, the market stalls become full of rustic offerings which are produced in an arid and rocky environment. This is the land of almonds, honey and lavender whose colours and fragrances combine with each other so well. Although it is mainly made up of a mass of small, local producers' stalls, the market in Apt is a thriving one. The shepherds' wives bring the "banon" cheese wrapped up in chestnut leaves and carefully arranged in a wicker basket. The bee-keeper sets out his pots of honey around an antique, straw bee-hive. The confectioner presents his candied melons, which have been macerating for hours in sugar, and is unconcerned about the competition from Aptunion who, on the outskirts of the town, confect enormous quantities of cherries destined to garnish fruit cakes throughout England. In winter, the truffle-hunters contribute sack-loads of truffles which grow in abundance in this part of the Vaucluse. The potters come down from the Luberon to sell their attractive, coloured pots, fruit of their inspiration and skill, which serve as a reminder that, in the last century, the inhabitants of Apt produced the original, marbled earthenware that can be admired in the archaeological museum.

After the market do not miss:

The Luberon and its old villages : Oppède-le-Vieux, Bonnieux, Ménerbes, Lacoste.
The Colorado Provencal, quarries of natural ochre and the old village of Roussillon.
A bike ride to Cereste along the old railway track which has been made into a cycle path.
The Albion plateau and its fields of lavender (in bloom at the beginning of July).

Arles

Arles offers one of the most impressive markets of Provence to match the size of its sprawling municipality. It extends for more than 2 kilometres on the pavements of the large boulevards which encircle the town. The rows of "micocouliers" provide generous shade for the colourful crowd drawn every Saturday morning by the incredible diversity of goods. In this greatly mixed community everybody can find what they are looking for: horse saddles and sheep collars for the Camarguais, chickens ready to have their throats slit in the moslem tradition, printed Provençal shirts, tellines (small shell-fish) which have been fished on the long, sandy beaches of the Rhône delta, Camargue bull steaks, handmade soap from Marseille oozing with olive oil and salad bowls made from light-golden olive wood. A colourful assortment of fruit and vegetables can be found alongside the famous, Arles "charcuterie", heavily seasoned with garlic. By setting off from the banks of the Rhône, you will firstly come across articles of clothing and large printed tablecloths and will then pass through the entire range of products which are grouped together one after the other along the boulevard to finally arrive at the flower stalls set up at the foot of the ancient city walls.

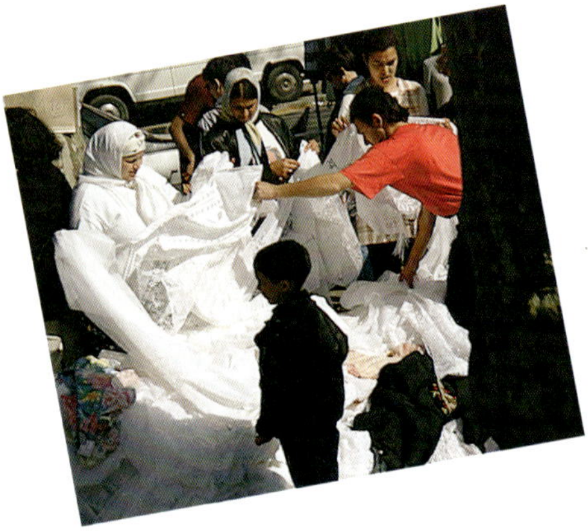

After the market do not miss:

The arena and the Roman theatre.
The church of St. Trophime, its Roman portal and cloister.
The archaeological museum "Arles antique".
The Camargue, its ponds and nature reserve.
Vincent Van Gogh museum.

Aups

The old village of Aups with its numerous fountains is situated on the road to the gorges de Verdon and is reached by going through untamed forests of oak trees. Here the entire male population is aroused by hunting. The boutique selling hunting gear has an imposing position in the middle of the village, next to the town-hall, the church and the café where the hunters, in camouflage combat dress, revel in recounting their last boar hunt whilst the old men in caps play endless games of cards. Thrush, stuffed with juniper berries, is still served at winter dinners. From November, truffles appear on the roots of oak trees and are brought back by the truffle hunters in dozens of kilos to the special, Thursday morning market. During the summer season, the more inquisitive holiday-maker will leave behind the congested, turquoise creeks and the Durance valley's golden melons to search in this luminous hinterland for a different, authentic Provence. Discover it and marvel at the quaintness of the village with its Saturday morning market, as pretty as it is small, sensibly set up in the cool shade of the enormous plane trees around the cenotaph.

How a salmi of thrush is prepared in Aups :
Take a well-hung thrush and cut off its feet. Do not clean it out.
Chop it up and add a few really ripe juniper berries and a little bacon. Spread this preparation onto a stale slice of bread from the previous day and put it in the oven. Serve it hot.

After the market do not miss:

A tour of the village: its fountains, ramparts, the clock-tower and its pretty bell-tower in wrought iron and the church of St. Pancrace which houses beautiful, 17 century paintings.
Villecroze: grottos, castle and underground lake, exotic gardens at the foot of the cliffs.
The sublime clifftop road along the Grand Canyon of Verdon.
Moustiers-Sainte-Marie and its famous earthenware.
The lake of St. Croix.

Grasse

On the Place aux Aires, for hundreds of years leather was beaten, tanned and softened in the main water duct which was in those days exposed to the open air. Today, Grasse is more occupied with cultivating flowers than with tanning leather. In the shafts of light from the former tanning areas edged with high, multicoloured facades, the flower stalls form a pretty crown around the fountain. In front of the harmonious curves of the old arcades, sellers of vegetables, spices, olives, candied fruits, cheese and "charcuterie" display their produce artistically to create one of the prettiest markets around. The seller of organic produce dispenses as many philosophical words as natural vegetables and the old lady who sells herbs and olive oil has been unfolding her trestle-table and stool for the last forty years in this same little place. A maze of little, narrow alleys descend towards the Place aux Herbes, which has a distinct South Mediterranean feel. At the foot of the townhall, the fish hall, a small, metallic, "belle-époque" style construction, spreads its refreshing shade over the shining shapes of the fish and shell-fish.

After the market do not miss :

The old, historic town (a circuit is indicated).
The cathedral, XII and XVII centuries.
The Fragonard museum, the marine museum and the museum of perfume.
A visit to the perfume factory.
The Gorges du Loup and the circuit of the villages set high up in the mountains : Gourdon, Cipières, Coursegoules.
The panoramic view from the village of Cabris.

Uzès

You may legitimately wonder why the Uzès market is included in a book about the markets of Provence when it is located in Languedoc. Let's just say that this market is so famous and so Provencal in spirit that nobody will condemn the liberty we have taken regarding its geographical position. La Place aux Herbes, bordered by irregular arcades and crenellated towers which emerge from the early morning mist, resembles a set specially designed to present a play entitled "the market". One stallholder will assure you that she has been selling second-hand clothes for twenty years and can guarantee that there is nobody in Uzès who hasn't bought something. The huge variety of goods can hardly be believed. Crockery sold by the kilo, rolls of printed material, wicker-work, hardware, the square is too small to accommodate everything and the stalls overflow onto the circular boulevard. Near the fountain, the cheese merchant shouts at the top of his voice: "It's not cheese, it's indulgence, that's what the good shepherd says!" The same good humour presides at the other markets on the Place aux Herbes: the day of the truffle at the end of January, the garlic market in June, the wine festival in August and the potters' market at Easter. Uzès certainly did not acquire its good reputation for nothing!

After the market do no miss:

A tour of the town (old staircases).
The church and the old organ.
The Pont du Gard.
Numerous walks along the Gardon or the Cèze, Lussan and the Concluses.
Nimes.
The potters in Saint-Quentin-la-Poterie.

Saint-Tropez

One could think that Saint Tropez would have lost its Provençal cheerfulness after having been invaded for the past forty years by an army of show-biz stars following in the footsteps of Brigitte Bardot, after its bombardment by Deutsch marks and dollars and after the repeated overcrowding of the port each year by the most enormous yachts, the loudest-mouthed show-offs and the most beautiful ships sailing under the Panamanian, Liberian or West Indian flags. But no! Lose yourself on a Tuesday or a Saturday under the plane trees of the market of La Place des Lices. Enjoy yourself browsing in the little market of La Place des Herbes which takes place every morning. Mix with the tourists round the port and look over the shoulders of the painters and caricaturists. You will notice that, by some miracle, the spirit of Saint Tropez is still Provençal. Indeed, as soon as you enter the tropézien alleyways you will be struck by their distinctive charm and even the flashy, polished cars proudly lined up at the edge of the market are a reminder of the undeniable macho side to the character of any self-respecting Provençal.

After the market do not miss:
The port, its fishing boats anchored under the shadow of the most beautiful yachts in the world.
The quays and the permanent "marché aux croutes" (a market of daubs).
The Anonciade museum, Neo-impressionist, Nabis and Fauvist painters.
The Port Grimaud marina.
The large beaches of Pampelonne and the customs officers footpath towards Escalet.
The interior of the peninsula, the mills of Paillas and the villages of Gassin and Ramatuelle.

Sunday

VAUCLUSE
Avignon (les remparts)
Camaret-sur-Aigues
Coustellet (summer)
Isle-sur-la-Sorgue
Monteux
St-Martin-de-la-Brasque (summer)

BOUCHES-DU-RHÔNE
Châteaurenard
Bouc-Bel-Air
La Ciotat
Gardanne*
Gignac-la-Nerthe
Jouques
Pélissanne
Vitrolles*

VAR
La Croix-Valmer (summer)
Le Muy*
Ramatuelle (summer)
Port-Grimaud (summer)
Saint-Cyr-sur-Mer
Vidauban*

ALPES DE HAUTE-PROVENCE
Mane
Reillanne
Saint-Michel-l'Observatoire

DRÔME PROVENÇALE
Grignan
Nyons
Saillans (été)

**twice weekly market*

Avignon

If you are frightened of travelling by plane but enjoy Arab markets, nothing could be simple : escape to the ramparts in Avignon between the Porte Limbert and the Porte Saint-Michel on a Saturday or Sunday morning for a warm Arabian welcome. You are greeted by the sound of oriental music diffused from huge loud-speakers by the guy selling C.D.'s and video-cassettes. You can choose the henna to give your hair pretty highlights, sesame seeds or curry powder and the spices for the couscous from a small mobile stall run by a child of twelve. The aluminium "cous-cousier" isn't far away, it is found with the stainless steel teapots and gilt-edged tea glasses. Stems of fragrant mint and coriander await those who have the acquired taste. Young, bearded men wearing white, cotton, crocheted skullcaps expertly tap the water-melons or compare the qualities of the different varieties of dried dates. Behind a mountain of watches selling at 50 francs and an assortment of shirts at 10 francs, material sold by the metre hangs like giant ties : dark serge for a pair of trousers for sir and brilliant, pink satin for a dress for madam. The sewing-machine to make the clothes and the gilted belts to complement them can be found on the neighbouring stall.

All the rest of the week, except Monday, "les halles" (the covered market) inside the city walls is open. The ambiance is less exotic but there is everything in the way of fresh produce.

After the market do not miss:

The Popes' Palace.
The Pont d'Avignon (Pont St. Bénézet).
The museums: Petit-Palais, Calvet, Angladon-Dubrujeaud.
Villeneuve-lès-Avignon: Fort St. André, Chartreuse.
A walk in the hills of "la Montagnette" or at the Pont du Gard.

L'Isle-sur-la-Sorgue

The Sorgue, a river whose waters are cool, clear and flow at a steady pace, gives charm to this little town which is surrounded by verdure and shade. The first inhabitants of L'Isle-sur-la-Sorgue were fishermen who lived in huts in the middle of the marshes. The fruits of their fishing, eel, crayfish, loach, trout and other fish were reserved for the pope and other nobility, then for the locals and finally for foreigners. A papal bull gave a franchise to inhabitants and strangers alike going to and from the market guaranteeing that nobody could be arrested unless the crime was lèse-majesty or murder. This franchise attracted a considerable number of people and the merchandise, free from all levy, was traded liberally. Primarily, everything that was produced locally in the numerous water-mills could be found, such as flour, oil, silk, blankets, woollen fabrics, shepherds coats, Avignon carpets, paper but also merchandise from far afield like wheat from Italy and even from the Levant. Today the town, whose activity is much reduced, regains life every Thursday and Sunday when all the roads are invaded by stallholders and at the weekends when it is transformed into the capital for antique dealers.

After the market do not miss:

Discover the town: the paddle wheels, Renaissance houses, the Campredon museum.
The Baroque church dedicated to Our Lady of the Angels.
The "brocante" village (during the weekend).
A walk where the waters divide.
1 km upstream you can descend the Sorgue in a canoe.
Fontaine-de-Vaucluse: perhaps the most important source in the world.

Every day

VAUCLUSE
Avignon (les halles)
Velleron (summer 18-20 h)*

BOUCHES-DU-RHÔNE
Aix-en-Provence
Marseille
Port-de-Bouc (except Monday)
St-Etienne-du-Grés
(summer in the evening)
Sénas (excep Sunday and
public holidays)

VAR
Bandol
La Seyne-sur-Mer
Puget-sur-Argens
Sainte-Maxime-sur-Mer
Toulon
*3 times weekly in winter
16 h 30 - 18 h 30

Aix-en-Provence

To enable the villeins of his castle in Vallabrègues to sell the produce from his vegetable gardens and orchards, king René made them a gift of the square, which was to become the market square (today Place Richelme). The king's stall was a large, stone table from which his vegetables were sold. Around this stall, meat, fish and all the other produce or agricultural implements were on offer to customers. The market was soon complemented by the covered grain market where the "mouliniers" came to stock up with cereals. After the Revolution kings disappeared but the square retained all its charm. In the shade of its plane trees, local producers come every single day, be it in summer or in winter, come rain or shine, to sell the fruits of their labour and also produce coming from further afield. Nothing but the freshest fruit and vegetables are on sale. Set back a little from the main market square, attractive displays of fish and shell-fish are to be found and, in addition, a botanical market.

Every Tuesday, Thursday and Saturday, Aix-en-Provence excels itself by multiplying the number of markets in the centre of town. There you will find the flower-sellers around the fountain on Place de l' Hôtel de Ville, the pretty "marché paysan" and the flea market on the Place de Prêcheurs and on the famous Cours Mirabeau, clothing and "artisanat" of all kinds.

Culinary speciality:
The Calissons of Aix (made from almond paste, candied melon and fruit syrup).

After the market do not miss:

A walk under the plane trees of the Cours Mirabeau.
Cathedral St. Sauveur, triptych of the burning bush by Nicolas Froment.
Granet Museum, Works by Paul Cézanne.
Hikes up the Sainte-Victoire mountain and accross the landscapes cherished by Cézanne.

Marseille, Le Prado

The parasols are neatly arranged in front of the austere facades of the buildings but it is the enterprising Mediterranean spirit of commerce that brings lively colour to the "Prado" market to vie with the "la Plaine" market for the title of the most beautiful market in Marseille. On all days of the week apart from Sunday it is a large market. However, on Friday it reaches monumental proportions when the flamboyant flower market adds its sprays of colours. Drowned by the crowd, the little "bourgeoises" of the district, dressed up to the nines hover and jostle feigning not to touch anything but pick up, for next to nothing, a little blouse or summer dress that looks as though it was bought in one of the smart boutiques on the rue Paradis. The background noise is assured by everything Marseille can invent by way of calls, enticements, interjections, onomatopoeias and of unbelievable sales patter recited, yelled or spouted in the inimitable local dialect.

Marseille has at least 19 food markets. The biggest stallholder markets are Le Prado (everyday except Sunday) and La Plaine (Tuesday, Thursday and Saturday morning). Then come those of La Place Sébastopol (Monday, Wednesday and Friday morning), of Cours Pierre Puget (Monday, Wednesday, Friday morning) of a Belle-de-Mai (Monday, Wednesday, Friday and Saturday morning) of Notre-Dame-du-Mont (Wednesday and Friday), of Boulevard Michelet (Thursday morning), of Canet (Tuesday and Thursday), of l'Estaque (Saturday morning), of Cours Julien (Wednesday and Friday), Velten and Capucins (every day 8 a.m. to 7 p.m.)

After the market do not miss:

The basilica of "La Bonne-Mère" and the panoramic view of Marseille.
The old port and the Panier district.
Boat trip to the isle of If.
Cassis and the "calanques" (creeks).

Sénas

People from the North who hurtle down towards "la grande bleue" do not imagine, when they pass the motorway exit "Sénas" on the "autoroute du soleil", that a few hundred metres away there is a small gem of a market. Every morning, in summer, but above all on Saturday, a large handful of local producers, with grandpa or grandma sometimes standing in, install themselves at the rear of their vans and transform the ordinary shade given by the plane trees on the parking area into a kaleidoscope. The tomatoes are not impeccable and impersonal like those from the greenhouses, they are even a bit deformed, but their flavour can only leave their bland rivals playing "catch up" ! A grandmother stuffs a bunch of carrots into your bag and with a smile, confides to you "Oh, ce marché, y' va tomber a zéro, c'est pas cher, on donne tout ici!" And the best of it is that she makes you a gift of the carrots. During this time, her neighbour, wisely sitting in the shade on her fold-up chair, shells beans for those who like pistou soup. Of course, in the region everyone knows the market and the folk from Aix or Salon do not hesitate to come here when they want to find really fresh produce picked from a family vegetable garden for next to nothing.

From 1st June until 30th September, every morning (except Sunday) but the most important day is Saturday from 9.30 a.m.
The rest of the year every Monday, Wednesday, Friday and Saturday.

After the market do not miss:
The grottoes and troglodytic dwellings in Calès, near Lamanon.
The nature trail in Lamanon.
The Empéri museum in Salon-de-Provence.
Rambles in the Alpilles or the Luberon (in summer take into account the existence of the "zones rouges" which are strictly out of bounds for walkers).

Toulon

If you like wonderful fruit and vegetables, freshly picked and inexpensive, attractively displayed in the Provencal light which filters through the leaves of the plane trees, the market in Toulon will enchant you. Its fame is well merited. From daybreak, the Cours Lafayette is entirely invested with an army of barrows full of fruit and vegetables, the produce of local vegetable gardens. The abundance of what is on offer does not leave much chance for those who want to get rid of produce which is no longer fresh or who want to ask high prices. “Allez, les clients, c'est sans bénéfice, c'est pour vous faire plaisir!”. It's a pagan cult in homage to saint asparagus, saint melon and saint strawberry. A high-priest of salads offers an extraordinary choice of greenery: “mesclun”, rocket, “méli-mélo”, “rougette”, chicory, endive, “colorosa”, “romaine”, “cheveux d'ange” (angel's hair), “caparice”, red or green lettuce, lambs' lettuce, dandelion, watercress… and, right at the end little fish stalls invite you to prepare a good Mediterranean fish soup. Meat is to be found a little out of the way, in the cool of the covered market (les halles).

After the market do not miss:

A boat trip of the harbour.
Marine museum.
Mont-Faron, memorial of the disembarkment, splendid view (cable car).
Hyères, a cruise to the Porquerolles and Port-Crau.

Fairs and markets with a special theme

Buis-les-Baro
Nyons
Banc
Orange
Carpentras
Apt
Lourmar
Gordes
Avignon
Pertuis
Cavaillon
Beaucaire
Arles
Salon
de Provence
Aix-en-Pro
Carry-le-Rouet
Marseille
Aubag

Fairs and markets with a special theme

Garlic markets:

In the heat and light of the third weekend of August, the smell of garlic, the glory of Provencal cookery, invades the centre of Piolenc and all the population lets its imagination and fantasy run wild in celebration of garlic for which the village boasts of being the capital. The producers have enormous pyramids of it on offer. White, pink or violet, garlands, tresses or bunches leave you in a quandary for choice but it is said that the very best, the strongest smelling and the most expensive is the red garlic or "moulinin" which is matured for fourteen months.

Garlic is an almost universal old wives remedy but doctors also recognise its innumerable virtues. In ancient times, the Egyptians distributed large quantities to the slaves who built their pyramids in order to give them strength. The Hebrews used it to protect themselves from viper bites and scorpion stings. The great Hippocrates prescribed it against cholera and the plague and Discorides recommended it to orators to help the voice. Still today, insect stings can be relieved by rubbing them with a clove of garlic, respiratory and blood circulation troubles can be treated by eating garlic spread and it is also said that a cold can be cured by rubbing the soles of the feet with garlic ! Garlic is found everywhere in Provence, but the best known garlic markets are:

Piolenc: 3rd weekend of August
Marseille: Cours Belsunce, everyday from mid-June to mid-July, associated with "teraillettes" (miniatures).
Uzès: 24th June for the feast of St. John.

Ail mince de peau, hiver court et beau!

Artisan is a word meaning craftsman and artist, and "artisanat" is the art of creating a useful and attractive object, pleasing to look at, to touch, to smell, to taste or to listen to. The Provençal spirit which is both imaginative and convivial is inherently suited to all forms of "artisanat". In every market in Provence there is an "artisanat" stall of some kind: bread made in the old-fashioned way, "fougasse aux lardons", nougats and spiced honey cake, olive and anchovy pastes and a thousand other preparations containing olive oil, garlic, honey and lavender, all to tempt your taste buds.

Artisanat

Je veux juste une bricole, c'est pour un petit cadeau!

Aubagne or Salernes clay, moulded or turned by a small group of local potters as well as a number of craftsmen from the North who have come to practise their craft under the blue, Mediterranean sky, is transformed into "tommettes" (miniatures), vases, jugs and even whistles, small bells and, of course, "santons" (crib figures). Leather and wool from the Camargue or Alpine herds are made into belts, bags, multicoloured or black skeins and hats for the Camargue "cowboys" whereas the printed cottons from the Tarascon area are made into Provençal shirts, tablecloths or gathered skirts. Olive wood makes admirable salad bowls as its golden colour blends so well with bright coloured lettuce, aubergines or peppers. Dried flowers are assembled with great flair to decorate straw hats or to make table decorations. Before your very eyes, the upholsterer will skilfully design a Provençal armchair. The basket-worker, who has amassed a dozen varieties of old willow canes each of a slightly different shade, will employ them to make the pretty baskets traditionally used for collecting cherries or potatoes or to create strange rattles which supposedly protect babies from evil spells cast by demons.

Principal "artisanaux" markets:

Aix-en-Provence, Cours Mirabeau: Easter weekend, May, June, September, October.

Avignon: Allées de l'Oulle throughout the Festival.

La Roque d'Anthéron: beginning of summer and 15th August. September, October.

The arrival of asparagus at the markets marks the beginning of warmer days. The asparagus harvesters, who rise at dawn, use long gouges to collect the delicious tips which poke their heads up towards the light. They have little nutritional value as they contain 92% water but their flavour is greatly appreciated by gourmets who impatiently await their appearance. The white variety, which is never exposed to the light, is the first to be harvested at the end of March. Then comes the green variety of the Midi, followed by the "Lauris" sought by the restaurateurs and finally the violet variety which is more fruity and fragrant.

Asparagus

Everyone has their own preference. In northern regions only the light-coloured varieties are eaten whereas in Provence the darker varieties are generally preferred. However, the last word is had by the thin, green, wild asparagus whose flavour marries so well with that of olive oil. You can search for it on scrubland but it is rarely found on sale. Asparagus does not like the sun, heat or dry air. The best are heavy, shiny and firm. If droplets appear when you cut the asparagus, it is a sign that it is very fresh and therefore tender. To maintain their freshness before cooking, treat them like cut flowers and put their stems in water. Peel them from the top downwards so that the fragile tip is not damaged. If you want an inexpensive treat, choose asparagus tips which have been broken off their stems. They may be less presentable but are just as good and much cheaper.

C'est dur, madame,
de gagner deux millions
par jour,
20 francs la botte!

At the end of April,
discover the asparagus market
in Mormoiron.

"Cowboys" mounted on their white horses and armed with tridents still splash their way across the "étangs" of the Camargue to round up the black bulls. And although horses are no longer used to plough the plains and the hill-sides of Provence, they are still an attraction at all of the regional "fêtes" as they participate in cavalcades and historical processions adorned in their decorative harnesses. Horseriding and equestrian events keep the love of horses alive in the region, which explains the astonishing number and importance of the horse, donkey and pony fairs.

Horse, Donkey and Pony fairs

Fontvieille, beginning of March.
Bellegarde, 1st Sunday of May and 2nd Sunday of November.
Forques, 1st weekend of September, foal market.
Uzès, 8 days after Bellegarde.
Oppède-le-Vieux, mid-April.
Bédarrides, May, Ascension.
Seyne-les-Alpes, 2nd Saturday of October.
Pertuis, June.
Mazan, Easter Monday.

There can be up to 400 animals at any one time. When, as in Fontvieille, the fair is held near an arena, the owners take the opportunity to show off the qualities of their beasts by making them gallop round and round the sandy ring. Donkeys are also on show at these markets. Courageous and enduring, they have accompanied shepherds over the centuries in the transhumance across the difficult routes of Haute-Provence, carrying material, food for the shepherds, salt for the ewes and even the new-born lambs. Since December 1995, the donkey of Provence breed which has a cross on its back and a coat which is a dove-grey bordering on a pink colour, is recognised by the stud farms as being as important as the breeds of Berry or of Poitou.

In the Maures mountains, autumn turns the leaves of the chestnut trees golden. The spiky shells, which release the beautiful, shiny chestnuts, fall from the lustrous bronze branches. Don't miss the chance to enjoy the great spectacle of autumn and the last fragrances of summer by visiting the chestnut markets and by organising a good "castagnade". And here is the recipe. Choose small chestnuts, because they are sweeter than the large ones, make a small incision in them and grill them in a pan which has holes in the bottom over a flame and not over embers. Make sure you have plenty of chestnuts and a fine Provençal rosé wine to accompany them. Bon appétit !

Chestnut markets

Collobrières,
last three Sundays in October.
La Garde-Freinet, Les Mayans,
Gonfaron and Pignans, variable dates
at the end of October,
beginning of November.

Two of my grandmother's tips:

To make roasted chestnuts more tender: as soon as they are cooked wrap them up in a tea-cloth or newspaper and leave them for five minutes. The steam will soften the flesh and make them easier to peel.

To make uncooked chestnuts easier to peel, make an incision around the chestnut deep enough to reach the skin and plunge them in boiling, salted water for three or four minutes.

Mangez des marrons, c'est naturellement bon!

There was a time when leather represented one of the principal riches of the region due to the existence of vast herds and to the abundance of water from the Rhône, the Durance and the Sorgue. Every village had its road of tanners. Bundles of skins cluttered up the embankment of the Rhône at the great Beaucaire fair. Avignon almost went to war with Villeneuve in order to hold its leather fair before that of its Languedoc rival. In Grasse, scented leather gloves launched the perfume industry.

Leather

Alpes de Haute Provence
St. Etienne les Orgues, July,
Seyne les Alpes, August.
Bouches du Rhône
Cassis, September. Maussane, Mai.
Mimet, June.
Drôme
La Garde Adhémar, May. Nyons, July.
Mirmande, August.
Var
Aups, August. Bandol, May and end
August. Lorgues, April and July.
Port Grimaud, April. Ramatuelle,
end August.
Vaucluse
Gordes, September.

This long tradition of tanners and leatherwork craftsmen still exists today. Many "marchés artisanaux" are devoted to leather, often combining it with jewellery, wool or wood. At these markets you will have great difficulty in choosing between selected blousons each one individually made and elegantly decorated with coloured motifs; belts embellished with interchangeable buckles and dyed in muted tones; elegant or rustic bags; sandals; wallets, which are hand-sewn and made to order; bracelets and other leather jewellery; and folding stools for walkers.

Tout cuir français, allez monsieur, n'hésitez pas!

Africa begins in Marseille but so too does the Orient and Oceania. A little visit to the Capucins market place will allow you to verify this. Amongst the merchants who vie for your attention, you will notice that many are not of Gallic descent. There is, therefore, a great variety of merchandise on offer: stringless green beans from Morocco, mangoes from the Ivory Coast, grapes from South Africa, taros (turnips) from Tahiti, ginger from Cambodia and chillies from Madagascar. However, you also find the familiar "champignons de Paris", and the asparagus is produced locally.

Exotic markets

And if you want to reach the soul of the markets of France's former colonies, their hubbub and their musky fragrance or, if you want to find a fruit or vegetable which you enjoyed whilst in the tropics, adventure a little further along the long Rue des Capucins. Thousands of different, exotic foods, the fragrance of spices and of mint, a mix of all colours of skin and of all accents, friendly bustling and disorientation awaits you.

Si vous n'avez pas de sous, c'est pas grave, je vous garde en otage!

Provence produces more than three-quarters of the cut flowers sold in France. From the month of February, the smell of mimosa wafts down the slopes of the Tanneron and enraptures the olfaction of the whole of France. Nice, which has specialised in the production and export of carnations and roses since the birth of the railway, proudly exhibits armfuls of flowers at the market of Saleya. Antibes, prides itself in producing magnificent roses and Grasse uses enormous quantities of roses to develop its famous perfumes.

Flower markets

You will come across fields of tulips at the foot of the Dentelles de Montmirail and, in autumn, immense fields of violet, yellow, mauve or white chrysanthemums appear. The wholesale market in Carpentras is one of the most important markets for flowers and plants in Europe. An abundance of quality flowers can be found at all the markets in Provence. Their colourful message always appeals to the heart and makes even the most humble market attractive.

The following markets merit special attention:

Nice, market of Saleya, specialising in cut flowers for export to the whole world.

Marseille, Le Prado, Friday; La Plaine, Wednesday.

Aix-en-Provence, Place de la Hotel de Ville, Tuesday, Thursday, Saturday. Place des Prêcheurs, Monday, Wednesday, Friday and Sunday.

Avignon, Place des Carmes, Saturday.

On the first Sunday of August, at the height of the summer heat, a shaded reach of the river Sorgue welcomes the prettiest flotilla of barges that you could imagine. On the cool, clear waters, all Provencal products come together and are attractively displayed on the traditional, flat-bottomed barges that the Sorgue fishermen have used for over a thousand years. The "Isliens" call these small, harmoniously designed craft "négo-chin" in memory of the dogs who drowned whilst accompanying their masters fishing.

The floating market of L'Isle-sur-la-Sorgue

The barges glide up and down stream in a colourful and spontaneous ballet responding to the calls from the clients dispersed on the river banks. There will be a barge with the white goat's cheeses, another one with pastries and others with "santons", fruit and vegetables exuding freshness, spiced loaf with almonds, black or white nougat, pink, fragrant garlic, herbes de Provence, dried, subtle coloured flowers, hens and their eggs in coops, wicker-work and pottery, scaled, handmade models of the "négo-chin", olives prepared in a thousand different ways and wine from the sunny hillsides of the nearby Luberon.

The only thing missing is the real fisherman's "négo-chin" laden with carp, perch, trout, pike and crayfish which were formerly the delights of the self-indulging Popes of Avignon.

Together with swallows and fluttering hearts, red fruits announce the spring. In Velleron, where the murmuring Sorgue still causes enamoured ducks to quack with delight, the fresh, fleshy and perfumed heart shaped strawberries ease the passage of time until the cherry season. Far from the hustle and bustle, simply equipped with a basket on the arm, the local housewives and happy tourists rediscover a little taste of bygone days. In the old village, attics have been cleared out to the great pleasure of lovers of bric-a-brac and antiques.

Strawberries

And on the shaded square, between rain showers and bright spells, the small local producers display their harvest. The varieties Garriguettes, Chandler, Belrubis, Surprises des halles or Miranda will have been picked very early in the morning. Standing in front of his agricultural van, Yves Lunel, a happily retired villager, knows that the best soil for the open field strawberries is to be found in the Plantiers area. Soon he will be picking his "Mara" strawberries which are named after Mr. Marionnet from Mily-la-Forêt who first cultivated them. This traditional strawberry, whose perfume is like that of the wild strawberry, should be bought in the evening at the "marché paysan" of Velleron.

The strawberry market in Velleron takes place at the beginning of May

Extracts taken from Mr. Gautherin
of "Le Provencal"

Fraises sublimes terribles, plein champ!

Between the Verdon and the Durance, the hills which surround Banon are covered with wild grasses in which the goats delight. From their perfumed milk, the shepherds extract a cheese which is smooth and flavoursome and which is dipped into "marc de raisin" before being folded in chestnut leaves and bound with raffia. At the Banon cheese festival, towards Whitsun, the little cheeses with their own particular shape and carefully arranged in boxes finish maturing under the cool shade of the plane trees.

Cheese markets

They transform into a white cream which is almost liquid and can be eaten with a little spoon. The Banon cheese, so called by Frédéric Mistral, is an old regional product as herds of goats have grazed on the undergrowth of the Haute-Provence since before the Roman occupation. They even maintain here that the Roman emperor Antonius, who was passing through, died of indigestion from having eaten too much of it! In Roaix, near to Séguret, on the first Sunday of July, the producers of goat's cheese from Picodon and the Vaucluse compete in a friendly, gastronomic contest held to ascertain the best cheeses in particular categories. Whatever your preference may be, you will find a cheese to suit your taste.

Market in Banon towards Whitsun and at Roaix on the first Sunday of July.

Si vous voulez rester jolies, mesdames, mangez de la brebis, c'est le berger qui vous le dit!

Sheep and transhumance form part of the traditional image of Provence. Although the great transhumance by foot has not been allowed since 1953, St. Rémy-de-Provence carries on its memory by organising a mini-transhumance on the road which encircles the town at the beginning of summer. On the plain of La Crau and in the Alpilles, flocks of 500 to 1000 still exist. To reduce the risk of contagion, the animals are no longer all assembled at the same time at the markets. However, an ovine fair does still exist in St. Christol-d'Albion at the beginning of August and there is a ram breeders' fair in St. Martin-de-Crau towards mid-March.

Sheep Fairs and Wool Markets

Rams and donkeys, in St. Martin-de-Crau towards mid-March.
Ovines, St. Christol-d' Albion, at the beginning of August.
Wool, in Forcalquier at the end of May and Gordes beginning of April.

This is where the shepherds meet. Here they buy rams, of course, but also umbrellas, hats and shepherds' knives, collars of sculpted wood adorned with small bells, branding-irons, donkeys and packsaddles, leads, halters, whips, etc… It is worth a visit to learn about the old trades before they disappear because today there are few young people who are prepared to do this tough, badly paid job.

As for the fleeces which used to be sold in Arles, their trade has disappeared but a few markets devote themselves to clothing and objects made from wool. The very colourful market of Forcalquier at the end of May where you can pick up a number of exclusive articles and that of Gordes, at the beginning of April, are worthy of special attention.

Perfectly adapted to the arid soil of the hinterland, from the beginning of summer the lavender spreads out its palette of monochrome mauves and violets. The straightness of its rows plays leap-frog with the hills creating an unbelievable interaction of perspective and colour. The screeching of the cicadas and the humming of the bees ensure a sonorous atmosphere whilst the penetrating perfume of the flower, crushed between your fingers, completes your exultation. At all the markets in Provence you will find little sacks of dried lavender to place in your linen cupboard, lavender essence of which only a few drops are needed to perfume your bath or to keep the moth at bay and bouquets of dried lavender to decorate your home.

Lavender and Honey

The amber-coloured honey is another joy of Provence. The beekeepers, often learned men, sell their honey at all the markets. They will let you compare the flavour of the lavender honey with that of the chestnut honey and taste their spiced loaves and home-made nougats. They are capable of healing all sorts of little health problems with grains of pollen, with royal jelly and propolis.

In the hills of the Cannes hinterland, the bees are pampered by numerous, bee-keeping fanatics who have a celebration at the end of April at a large honey market held under the leafy arbour of Mouans-Sartoux. Go and meet them to savour the many flavoured and coloured honeys. They will talk to you about these fascinating insects which patiently accumulate the spoils they have collected religiously flower by flower to give us this treasure: honey.

Honey markets: Mouans-Sartoux at the end of April, an itinerant market held in July depending on the year at either Quinson, Riez or Moustiers-Sainte-Marie. At the end of September or beginning of October in Mimet and in Roquebrunne-sur-Argens at the beginning of October.

Christmas draws near. The mistral frays the whisps of clouds in the clear, blue sky. With whetted appetites, Provençaux mouths begin to water in expectation just like Alphonse Daudet's dom Balaguère in "the three low masses" and all hasten to the Christmas markets in order to get ready for the "gros souper" (the Christmas eve supper). Arles opens the Yuletide market season at the end of November, Avignon follows in its footsteps and is soon followed by Coustellet and Rognes. At the end of each week in December, you will find Christmas markets dedicated to Christmas presents and decorations and above all delicacies for Christmas eve.

The Christmas markets

Indeed, Provencal tradition requires that there be thirteen desserts which each have a hint of peasant frugality: candied citrons, black and white nougat packed with pine kernels, hazelnuts, pistachio nuts and almonds and then the "fougasse" flavoured with orange blossom and with a trickle of freshly pressed olive oil, quince jam with grape must, and dates stuffed with marzipan. However, the traditional dried cod has now been replaced by more expensive and refined products: game, foies gras, ducks, geese, turkeys and capons, ceps and chanterelles, smoked salmon, oysters and shell-fish, fine wines, chocolate logs, juicy mangoes without forgetting the truffles, the gastronomic "black diamond" that the folk from Marseille from all walks of life rush to buy at the Rognes market.

***Avec un peu de sel,
et un petouillon
d'armagnac pour manger
avec le foie de canard...***

"Ten olives a day, keep the doctor away". Olives are so very much a part of the landscape that it is customary to consider that Provence's boundaries are coextensive with the culture of olives. Whilst the olive straight from the tree is inedible because of its bitterness, with simple, basic processes using ash or soda, salt, fresh water and natural seasonings they can be confectioned in a multitude of different ways. Each market in Provence offers an infinite assortment of olives which are served with big, holed, wooden ladles. "Picholines" seasoned with fennel, crushed olives from the valley of Les Baux, plain, black olives from Nyons, olives stuffed with anchovies, piquant olives, offer something for everyone's taste.

Olives

Pour Toussaint, l'olive à la main, pour Noël l'huile nouvelle!

"I cannot sympathise with you for having hardly any butter in Provence as you have such admirable oil". (Mme de Sévigné).

Here nobody gets confused between the "picholine" from the Gard and the "salonenque" of Salon which are eaten green, the "blanquette" of Carpentras that adds flavour to oil, the fragile "grossane" of Les Baux and the "tanche" from Nyons whose flesh is delicate and full of flavour and which is eaten when it is black, the "verdale" of the Bouches du Rhône and the half a dozen varieties of the Var. In December, each mill produces its own distinctive oil. The olive oils from the Alpilles and those from Nyons are protected by an "appellation contrôlée" which guarantees their quality. At the "Alicoque" festival in February, tasters dip a freshly toasted crouton into the new olive oil to savour the produce. Jeanne Calment, the most senior member of the human race, once confided: "I don't have any wrinkles because all my life I've looked after my skin with olive oil and with just a small puff of powder to finish off."

On three Sundays in February, the little port of Carry-le-Rouet becomes the gourmand capital for those who enjoy sea urchins. From these delicious "sea hedgehogs" or "sea chestnuts" they extract the pretty coloured star found at the bottom of the shell. The fishing boats bring barrels of sea urchins to the quayside and the fishermen sell them by the tray load. They are then savoured, with a squeeze of lemon, at tables which have been set out for the occasion on the rocks or on the jetty.

The Oursinades (Sea Urchin tasting)

It is said that male and female sea-urchins have a very prickly relationship! So to allow them to reproduce in all tranquillity, it is only permitted to fish them from November 1st to March 30th. It is, therefore, in January and February that the "oursinades" are held in Carry-le-Rouet, in Sausset-les-Pins and in Carro. However, if you are in the region in summer, you will discover the "sardinades" (sardine tasting), the "thonades" (tuna fish tasting) or the "moulades" (mussel tasting). So join in these gourmands markets and enjoy yourselves.

"Oursinades"
3 Sundays in February
in Carry-le-Rouet. Equally,
during the same period
in Sausset-les-Pins and in Carro.

Un festin, je vous le dis!

The evening market in Velleron stands out amongst the numerous "marchés paysans" which sprout up in the remotest villages during summer. Although it is small in size, this farmers' market which is held each evening enjoys a great reputation. Only farm produce is sold here. It does not take place in the streets but in an enclosure on the outskirts of the village. Before it opens, the farmers from round about line up their little vans one next to the other with the rear turned towards the central alley.

The farmers market at Velleron

C'est ma récréation le marché, ce soir il faut aller à la cueillette.

After having carefully displayed their goods on trestle tables, they sit down on the benches inside their vehicles and chat with their friends as they wait for the official to blow his whistle to signal that the market is open to the public. From the size of the vans it is obvious that only small quantities are for sale; one producer may only have three dozen bundles of asparagus whereas the next may only have twenty odd cabbages. Each producer simply brings that which he has freshly picked just before coming. The rich, surrounding plain carefully cultivated and protected from the Mistral by hedges of cypress trees and permanently irrigated by the little streams coming from the Sorgue river provides, on a daily basis, fruit and vegetables of irreproachable freshness. Everyone in the region knows about this market and many regulars come specially to Velleron to fill up their baskets with fruit and vegetables that the local farmers have lovingly cultivated for them.

The farmers' market in Velleron:
in summer, every evening from 6 p.m. except Sunday and public holidays.
from October, Tuesday, Friday and Saturday from 4.30. p.m. except public holidays.

Cézanne, Matisse, Seurat, Picasso, Van Gogh are amongst the most famous on the long list of 19th and 20th century artist-painters who found inspiration in Provence for their master pieces. A visit to the Annonciade museum in St. Tropez clearly illustrates how the light in Provence fascinated so many modern painters. It's the same fascination which is at the origin of a multitude of small and large paintings that you will come across at the festivals of painting which are held here and there in Provence during the summer.

Painters in the street

Painters in the street:
Mollans-sur-Ouvèze the weekend following the 14th July.
Equally, permanent market of drawings and paintings on the quays of St. Tropez throughout the tourist season.
Gigondas, painters in the street, at the end of July and in Beaumes-de-Venise at Easter.

Mollans-sur-Ouvèze, at the foot of the Mont Ventoux, has made it an annual institution. At the weekend following the 14th July, all the roads of the village are transformed into picture galleries. Perhaps you will be lucky enough to discover an unknown artist of genius whose painting you will take home with you to complete and enrich your personal gallery...

Every morning, on the Quai des Belges in Marseille, a theatrical performance is improvised. It is produced and acted by the troop of fishermen from Marseille and their priceless wives, daughters or companions. The fishing boats are moored at the quayside and discharge their load of innumerous, multicoloured, Mediterranean fish which are still very much alive. While the men continue to unravel the fish from the nets, the women put to good use their superb, Marseille accent to call the attention of the customers and to vaunt, in chosen words, the merits of their merchandise.

The Fish market

Just enjoy a sample which is best left in French (spoken in a Provençal accent).

- Vé, les clients, venez voir, que j'ai tout de beau ce matin
- Ah les belles galinettes, regardez que c'est beau! c'est tout vivant!
- Elle est folle, Ninou, elle vend le vivant au prix du mort!
- Regardez le maquereau, il a la queue d'un homme de 20 ans!
- Allez Monsieur venez voir qu'on vous les prépare!
- Allez, ça vient ma nine, combien vous en voulez, la mamie?
- Vé les clients, mangez du poisson! que la viande ça rend maboule!
- Ah, qu'elle bouge, qu'elle bouge, la sole vivante, profitez, 20 francs si vous la voulez, ça me fait de la place!
- Allez, 10 francs la bleue, la vraie, allez, 10 francs, tant pis, 10 francs les dernières, il faut les finir!
- Ça fait du bien de manger du poisson, c'est pour ça que nous avons de si belles cervelles, té!

Fish market, every morning,
Quai des Belges,
in the old port of Marseille.
Not to be missed for
any reason whatsoever!

The Potters Markets

Provençal potters have inherited an old artistic tradition which seems to be etched in the clay of all Mediterranean countries. A cohort of craftsmen, often from the north, have fled their dull native soil to settle down in sunlit Provencal villages. They combine their talent with that of the local potters resulting in an unprecedented wealth of artefacts: santons made from Aubagne clay, pipes from the white clay of St. Quentin-la-Poterie, polychromatic earthenware of Moustiers-Sainte-Marie, miniatures from Marseille, the Salernes red, hexagonal floor tiles, jugs, salad bowls, decorated tableware,

musical pipes, small bells, flower vases transformed into works of art by the technique of the inspired craftsmen and small statues or sculptures which are simply created for their artistic appeal. The potters often choose to live far away from the towns in pretty hamlets in the garrigue, miles from anywhere. This is fine for the quality of life and for inspiration but not for business... Therefore, they organise a great number of potters' markets amongst which the following are included:

Dieulefit, every other year, in spring.
Bandol, Bonnieux and Uzès, over the Easter weekend.
Arles, mid-May.
Avignon, end of May, Place du Palais des Papes.
Cadenet, mid-June.
St. Quentin-la-Poterie, mid-July.
Sault, 15th August.
Séguret, end of August.
Aubagne, every other year in August.
Cassis, 3rd weekend of September.

Santons are only found in Provence. A "santoun" in Provençal means a little saint. They are the expression of a naive faith which is deep-rooted and fervent. To understand this tradition a little better, listen to the santons' pastorale which relives the wonder of the shepherds, the kindness of the ox and ass, the nastiness of the innkeeper, the avarice of the rich and the awkwardness of the huntsman. All the everyday activities of a Provençal village are represented in the form of a santon. Each year the santon craftsmen invent new trades or new poses to enrich this large family of which "lou ravi", the fishmonger, the old man, the miller, the knife-grinder, the poacher and the policeman top the bill.

The Santon markets

The santon markets at the top of the Cannebière in Marseille and those in Aubagne and in Aix-en-Provence run from the beginning of December late into the evening. Children and adults alike place the figurines they need to complete their cribs in their little baskets. If you are not in Provence during the Christmas period, in summer you will find santons at the "artisanaux" markets and above all in Aubagne where santons are on sale on the Cours Maréchal Foch. If you would like to visit a santon workshop, you will find them in Aix and in Aubagne where the craftsmen will be delighted to satisfy your curiosity.

The Santon markets in Marseille, Aix-en-Provence and Aubagne are held every day throughout December and January, and in Aubagne during the summer.

Allez, on profite, allez on se sert, on se sert!

This market, which is one of the most colourful and picturesque in existence, has for nearly 200 hundred years traditionally taken place in Buis-les-Baronnies on the first and second Wednesday of July and during all this time nothing has changed. At the crack of dawn, the farmers come to the Ouvèze dyke, overladen with bundles ("bourras") of beige canvas which are filled with the sweet-smelling dried flowers and which are piled up in their vans, hand-carts or old cars which have ladders as roof racks. Immediately, the early morning air is filled with the mellow perfume of the linden blossom. Whilst all await the municipal weigher and his Roman scales, the sun appears and transforms the linden flowers into golden crowns which spill over from the enormous round, generous bundles.

The Linden Blossom market

Then the buyers appear to scrutinise the quality and freshness of the batches. The "petit",whose flowers are very fragrant and abundant but are not much to look at, will be sold for less than the "Benivay" whose colouring is more appealing. The "papés", who have done hours and hours of picking in the full sun, sit under the plane trees and calculate their profits. In the warm, filtered light which sinks its rays into the fragrant dust, enormous loads of flowers, whose colour is a soft, bright green, are boldly seized, gathered together, weighed and loaded while the photographers buzz like bees around a honeypot.

Linden markets:
1st and 2nd Wednesday
in July in Buis-les-Baronnies.
Other markets less important
in June and July in Mollans,
Vaison-la-Romaine, Villefranche.

If you happen to pass within 100 metres of the bar l'Univers in Carpentras on a Friday morning between November and March, you probably won't notice anything unusual. Then a subtle, unforgettable, wafting fragrance overcomes you and you know for sure that you are standing at the gateway to paradise. The Perigord truffle, the true tuber melanosporum, the black diamond, which has honoured the table of gastronomes for the past 4000 years is commonly called "la rabasse". In winter, it is Carpentras and Richerenches which become European capitals of the rabasse. At the break of dawn, all the "rabassiers" (truffle hunters) from the surrounding countryside, the brokers and restaurateurs get together for the ceremony of truffle dealing.

The Truffle Market

Business is discussed calmly. It' s the festival of silence. Buyers and producers know each other well and know what they are about. Their nostrils evaluate the product, a little scratch with the finger-nail confirms their expectation and small pieces of paper, accepted as bills of exchange, change hands. The next act is played at the Roman scales where the truffles are duly weighed and then stuffed into large canvas sacks. The last episode takes place around the tables in the café. Cheques and crisp 500 franc notes are taken from the brokers' bags and disappear into the hunters' pockets. It' s done quickly, precisely and by 10 o' clock it' s all over.

This is a stock-exchange usually reserved for professionals but nobody prevents you from taking the risk of approaching the rabassiers who wait for you on the pavement. At least permit yourself the poor man's pleasure of sniffing the fragrant, black tubers, and fingering them. If you are very audacious you can push your luck and ask them to stick a knife in a truffle to see what it' s like inside. Be aware that you are playing an exciting game but one full of pitfalls. You will often find that lower grade truffles without any flavour are slipped into a batch of good quality ones. They may be musky or mouldy, look very much like the genuine article but are not nearly as good. They may be damaged, slightly soft and rolled in a deliciously fragrant clay or even, heaven forbid! Chinese truffles with smooth skins, clandestine immigrants in “ la belle Provence ”. Fortunately, not all rabassiers are crooks and when you are savouring your scrambled-eggs with truffles you would give anything to have taste buds in the pit of your stomach and thus prolong a far too fleeting pleasure.

Sunday before Christmas,
truffle day in Rognes.
Mid-January, Mass celebrating
the truffle in Richerenches
and truffle day in Uzès.
December to March, truffle market
on Saturday in Aups.

At the beginning of the century, some 400 basketworkers practised their trade in Vallabrègues. In other words all the village made baskets. This activity was steadily developed as the fruit producers, increasing their production, demanded more and more baskets for the picking or transport of the fruit. Situated on an island on the Rhône, a short distance from the marshlands of the Camargue where the willow grows in abundance, Vallabrègues has become the capital of basketwork. Once a year on the second weekend of August, Vallabrègues, which today can count its basketworkers on the fingers of one hand, proudly and enthusiastically relives this era.

The Basketwork market

Il faut oser tresser l'osier pour laisser au moins un panier à l'éternité.

Seated under the plane trees, the basketworkers weave and sell a multitude of lovely baskets in warm light and dark colours. A large number of the villagers dig out of their cupboards outfits worn during the last century by their grandfathers and grandmothers. The hardy life of the willowcutters, who spent the winter in the Camargue, is faithfully reconstructed. All the houses in the village are decorated with baskets, wickerwork of all shapes and sizes, cases and old tools. At the end of the afternoon, when the golden light falls and slips itself obliquely under the plane trees, a large parade of old wagons hitched up to sturdy work-horses and laden with mountains of baskets makes its way around the alley which encircles the village re-enacting the return of the willowcutters.

Achevé d'imprimer en Avril 1998
Dépôt légal à parution

Imprimé en C.E.E.